The Peace Corps—
Making a Difference in the World

written by Mary Kaiser Donev

October 14, 1960. 2:00 a.m.

Rarely do we know the exact moment a dream is born.

Seldom does a dream change the world.

Only once in the 20th century did such a dream become reality.

It was named the Peace Corps.

On that October night in 1960, Senator John F. Kennedy should have been sleeping. The reporters who were traveling with him had decided nothing more would be happening that day on Kennedy's campaign for the presidency. They all left for their hotels and went to sleep.

Not Kennedy.

He knew that thousands of college students awaited him at the University of Michigan. He hadn't written out a formal talk, but he knew exactly what to say to them.

He spoke from his heart about the responsibility of being an American. He asked the students how many would be willing to serve their country and promote peace by working in developing countries around the world.

KENNEDY

The students were so moved that they started a petition. More than 1,000 people signed it. They were saying, Yes! We are willing to be part of making the world a better place. Let's get this program started.

Kennedy won the election and was sworn in as president on a cold January day a few months later. Again, he talked about his dream of taking all that was right and good about America and sharing it with the world. He dared all Americans to reach out to those who were distressed and in despair.

He was insistent in his speech to the nation that day. "To those peoples in the huts and villages of half the globe struggling to break the bonds of mass misery, we pledge our best efforts to help them help themselves...

"And so, my fellow Americans: ask not what your country can do for you—ask what you can do for your country," Kennedy continued. "My fellow citizens of the world: ask not what America will do for you, but what together we can do for the freedom of man."

Within weeks, the new president signed an order establishing the Peace Corps to "promote world peace and friendship."

Americans began to join the Peace Corps in small numbers. After several months of training, the first 51 volunteers arrived in Ghana, Africa in the stifling August heat. They surprised everyone who greeted them at the airport by singing the Ghana national anthem in the native language called *Twi*!

Within two years, thousands of volunteers were stationed in dozens of countries around the world.

What the Peace Corps demanded of volunteers would be hard—two years of service in a foreign country, thousands of miles from family and friends. The volunteers would receive no pay—just money for their food, housing, and transportation.

That didn't discourage the dream.

The volunteers were speechless when they saw crops that had been shriveled from drought. They knew that millions of people were suffering from hunger and were in need of medical care. These poor conditions encouraged the volunteers to want to help even more!

There is a saying, "Give a man a fish and you've fed him for a day. Teach a man to fish and you've fed him for a lifetime."

Peace Corps volunteers understood that giving hungry people food was a temporary solution. They had to help the people learn to take better care of themselves and their families. Volunteers gave all that they had—their energy, their knowledge, and their skills.

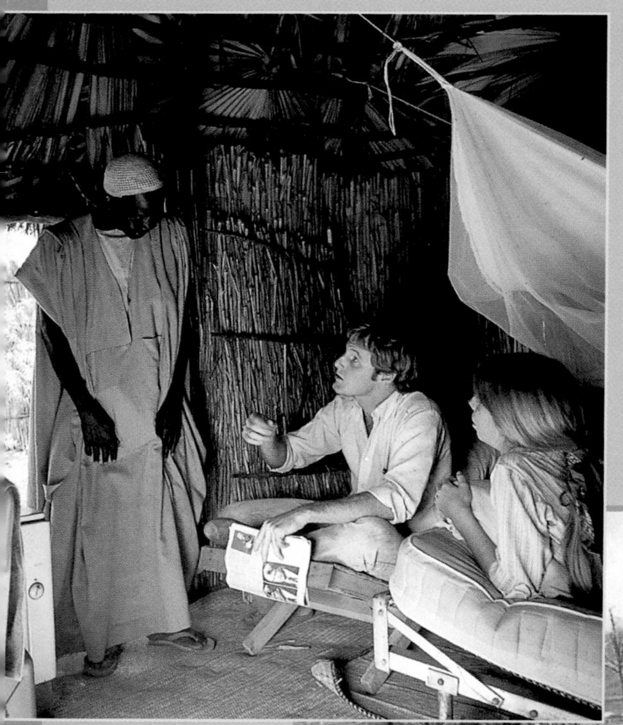

Those who knew about agriculture showed farmers better ways to irrigate their crops so that the plants wouldn't die from bad weather. Teachers shared knowledge with each other and with children in the classrooms. Doctors not only worked with the sick, but taught others how to become better doctors and nurses. Engineers worked to help villagers get clean water to drink.

When each volunteer's service ended and they returned home to the United States, they left behind a changed village and a legacy of hope.

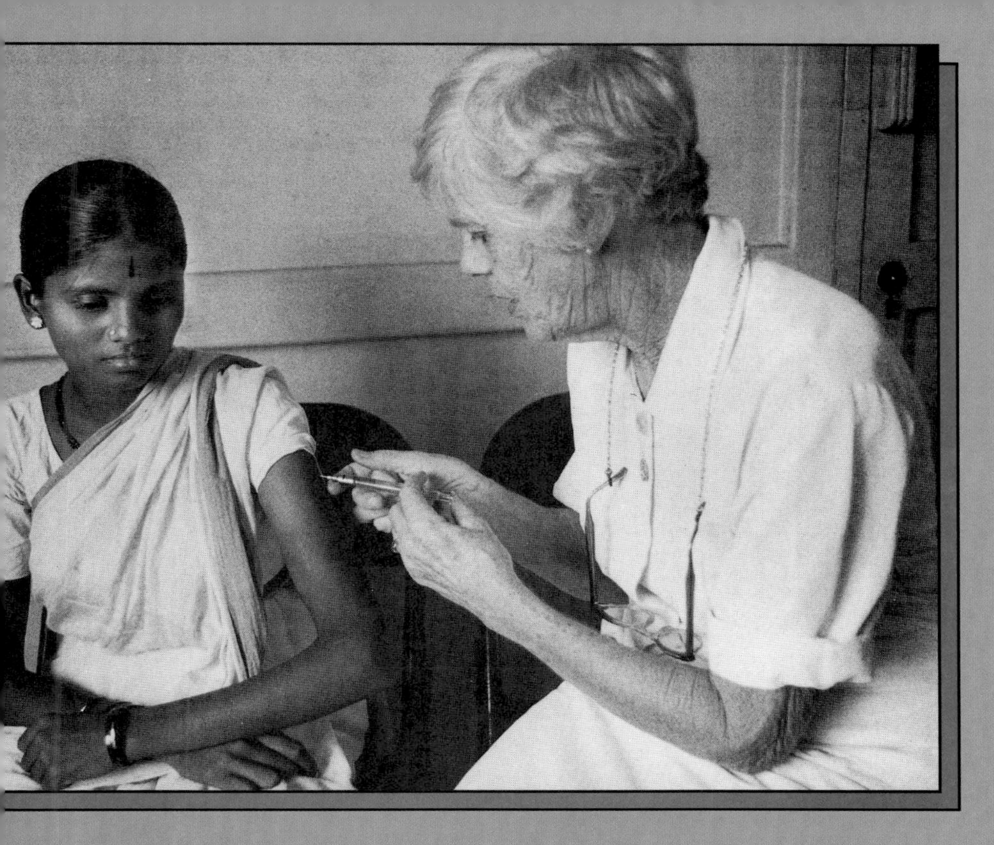

Although it was Kennedy's concept that began the Peace Corps, the dream did not end when he was assassinated in 1963.

Volunteers continued to sign up. They believed in the president's vision that the efforts of a few people making a difference could bring the promise of world peace.

They call it "the toughest job you'll ever love." Over 150,000 people have volunteered and have worked in more than 130 countries.

People as young as eighteen can join the Peace Corps, and there is no age limit on retirement. The oldest Peace Corps volunteer ever was 86 years old when he finally returned home!

Some husbands and wives volunteer together. Some have children that were born while they were living and working overseas.

As needs change, the Peace Corps develops programs and services to accommodate them. One current Peace Corps program sends volunteers to help out after natural disasters, such as earthquakes or floods.

Children in elementary and junior high schools are also involved. The World Wise Schools program matches Peace Corps volunteers with children in United States classrooms. Each volunteer corresponds with the students and shares experiences. He or she also gives students an inside look at the life and challenges facing people in other countries. The students sometimes offer their own ideas of what might work to improve life in a particular village.

In 1996, President Clinton honored the first group of volunteers ever to serve in the Peace Corps. This group, who had left for Ghana thirty-five years before, were introduced to a new group about to leave for the same country!

Former President Ronald Reagan explained why people join the Peace Corps and take part in the "toughest job they'll ever love":

"Each one of us is responsible for building the society we want. Peace Corps volunteers do that with people-to-people exchanges, using their energy, their spirit, and their creativity to solve problems. This is the American way. Once we see a need, we want to serve—even when the neighbor we reach out to help is halfway around the world."